Comprehensive Guide to Peptides:

From Basics to Advanced Applications

Tony Peptide

TABLE OF CONTENTS

Introduction to Peptides

Hey there, health enthusiasts!

Welcome to the exciting world of peptides! If you're reading this, I know you're not just curious—you're ready to level up your health game, and I'm pumped about that! Peptides are like tiny biological wizards that can unlock your body's natural healing powers. These small chains of amino acids are the secret sauce behind a lot of the cutting-edge wellness breakthroughs you're hearing about today. Whether you're looking for faster recovery, better sleep, balanced hormones, weight loss, or sharper mental clarity, peptides could be your new go-to.

Peptides are chains of amino acids, the building blocks of proteins. But here's what makes peptides special: they are small enough to act on specific receptors in the body, making them highly targeted and efficient. Over the years, peptides have become recognized for their potential to treat everything from injuries to metabolic disorders and anti-aging effects. In therapeutic settings, they help the body recover, heal, and improve functions that decline with age, such as metabolism, tissue regeneration, and hormone production.

This guide highlights how peptides are used to promote healing, burn fat, boost muscle growth, and improve cognitive function. **Peptide therapy**—which is about optimizing the body's natural processes through the use of synthetic or naturally occurring peptides—has been a revolutionary development in health and fitness. Whether you're looking at muscle-building peptides like **Ipamorelin** or **CJC-1295**, or fat-burning ones like **Semaglutide** and **Tirzepatide**, peptides work by either stimulating hormone release or interacting with specific cells to achieve precise, predictable results.

How to Prepare and Inject Peptides

Now, let's get into the hands-on part. You've got your peptides, but how do you actually prepare and inject them correctly? This step is critical—doing it right ensures you get the maximum benefits from your peptide while avoiding contamination or mistakes. So, let's break it down.

The Essentials: What You'll Need

Before you begin, here's your must-have list:

- **Alcohol prep pads** – Essential for sterilizing everything.

- **Bacteriostatic water** – This is what you'll use to reconstitute (mix) your peptides.

- **Peptide vial** – Peptides often come in freeze-dried (lyophilized) powder form.

- **Syringes and needles** – Different sizes for drawing water and injecting the peptide.

- Sharps container – Safe disposal for used needles.

According to the **Peptide Guide**, the most common dilution involves mixing **1-2 mL of bacteriostatic water** with the peptide powder, but this depends on the peptide's concentration.

Step-by-Step: Reconstituting Your Peptide

This is where you turn that freeze-dried powder into a usable liquid form. It's a simple process, but it needs to be done right.

1. **Sterilize everything:** Clean your hands and wipe down your workspace. Sterilize the tops of the peptide and bacteriostatic water vials with an alcohol prep pad.

2. **Draw up bacteriostatic water:** Using a large syringe, carefully draw up the appropriate amount of bacteriostatic water (usually 1-2 mL,

depending on your peptide). Insert the needle into the bacteriostatic water vial, draw slowly, and avoid air bubbles.

3. **Inject into the peptide vial**: Insert the syringe into the peptide vial at a slight angle, aiming for the side of the vial to avoid blasting the peptide directly. Let the water trickle in slowly to prevent foaming or excessive agitation. No shaking! Let the peptide dissolve naturally—if needed, give it a gentle swirl to help things along.

The guides from **Peptides.org** recommend paying attention to the correct dosage, as improper mixing can affect the potency and effectiveness of the peptide.

Drawing and Injecting Your Dose

1. **Switch to an insulin syringe:** This is for injecting the peptide. Insulin syringes are small and precise, perfect for subcutaneous injections.

2. **Clean your injection site:** Pick a spot like your abdomen, thigh, or upper arm. Wipe it down with an alcohol pad.

3. **Draw up the peptide:** Stick the syringe into the vial, draw the correct amount, and flick out any air bubbles.

4. **Inject subcutaneously:** Pinch the skin and insert the needle at a 45-degree angle. Inject slowly and steadily, then dispose of the needle safely in your sharps container.

The guides stress the importance of rotating injection sites to avoid irritation or scar tissue buildup.

Aftercare and Storage

Once injected, store any reconstituted peptides in the fridge to preserve their potency. Most peptides will last several weeks when stored properly, but always check the specific instructions for your peptide. And remember to monitor your injection site for any unusual reactions—slight redness is normal, but anything more significant should be checked out.

Peptides, which are now used for everything from performance enhancement to anti-aging treatments, have a fascinating history. They didn't just pop up overnight—this is the result of decades of research, breakthroughs, and a deeper understanding of how our bodies work. Let's take a look at how peptides evolved into one of the most talked-about therapies in modern health and wellness.

The Early Days: Medical Breakthroughs

The story of peptides begins with a medical miracle—**insulin**. Back in the 1920s, Frederick Banting and Charles Best made history when they discovered that insulin, a peptide hormone, could be used to manage diabetes. This was a game-changer for medicine, proving that peptides could be harnessed to treat serious conditions. Insulin therapy saved countless lives and opened the door for other peptide therapies.

In the **1960s**, **Human Growth Hormone (HGH)** became another milestone in peptide history. HGH was originally extracted from the pituitary glands of cadavers, which made it rare and expensive. But it was a critical treatment for children with growth disorders, showing the incredible potential of peptides to influence growth and development. It wasn't until the **1980s**, when synthetic HGH was developed using recombinant DNA technology, that HGH became widely available. This advancement was huge—not just for treating growth disorders but also for anti-aging and athletic performance.

Peptides in the Fitness World

The **1970s and 1980s** saw peptides step into the world of sports and fitness. As steroids were becoming increasingly controversial (and illegal in many sports), athletes began turning to peptides as a safer, more natural way to enhance performance. **GHRP-6** and **GHRP-2** were among the first peptides used to boost growth hormone levels, helping athletes recover faster, build muscle, and improve endurance without the same risks associated with steroids.

By the **early 2000s**, peptides like **BPC-157** and **TB-500** became recognized for their healing and regenerative properties. These peptides were originally used in medical research, particularly for their ability to speed up recovery from injuries, reduce inflammation, and support tissue repair. As their benefits became more widely known, athletes and fitness enthusiasts started using them to bounce back faster from injuries and improve overall physical performance.

The Modern-Day Peptide Revolution

Today, peptides are more than just performance enhancers—they're used in everything from **metabolic disorders** to **cosmetic applications** like skin rejuvenation. The **Research Peptides Guide** talks about how peptides are now designed to mimic or enhance specific biological functions, leading to what we call "designer peptides."

For example, **Semaglutide**—originally developed to treat Type 2 diabetes—has now found a home in the weight-loss world due to its powerful ability to reduce appetite and improve insulin sensitivity. On the flip side, **PT-141** (Bremelanotide) was initially studied for its ability to stimulate melanocytes (for tanning) but is now used as a treatment for sexual dysfunction.

What's most exciting is that we're only scratching the surface of what peptides can do. From **anti-aging** to **neuroprotective** treatments for diseases like Alzheimer's, peptides are becoming a cornerstone of health and wellness therapies. The potential of peptides goes beyond just living longer—it's about extending your healthspan, the number of years you can live actively and vibrantly

4

Peptides vs. Steroids

Alright, here's a question I get all the time: **Should I use peptides or steroids?** Both have their benefits when it comes to building muscle, speeding up recovery, and enhancing performance, but they work in very different ways. If you're weighing the options, it's crucial to understand how each one affects your body and what the long-term risks and rewards are.

How Peptides Work

Peptides are short chains of amino acids that act as signaling molecules in your body. They don't replace your body's hormones like steroids do; instead, they trigger specific biological processes to help your body function more efficiently. For example, peptides like **GHRP-2** and **Ipamorelin** stimulate the release of

growth hormone by interacting with receptors in the pituitary gland. This helps your body build muscle, burn fat, and recover from workouts faster—all by encouraging your body to produce more of its own natural hormones.

Because peptides are so targeted, they tend to have fewer side effects than steroids. They're designed to hit specific receptors and pathways, which means you can get the results you're after without throwing your entire endocrine system out of whack.

How Steroids Work

Steroids, on the other hand, are synthetic versions of hormones like **testosterone**. They flood your body with artificial hormones, which can lead to rapid muscle growth and strength gains, but they also come with a big list of potential side effects. Steroids work by binding to **androgen receptors** in your body, increasing protein synthesis and promoting muscle growth. But because they affect your entire hormonal system, they can cause long-term damage if not used properly.

Steroids have a reputation for delivering fast results, and that's true—they can help you pack on muscle quickly.

But the trade-off is that they often come with severe side effects, like liver damage, cardiovascular issues, and a disrupted natural hormone production. Over time, your body may stop producing its own testosterone, leading to problems like **testosterone suppression** and a need for post-cycle therapy (PCT) to restart your body's natural hormone production.

Peptides: The Natural Advantage

When comparing peptides and steroids, peptides have a major advantage in terms of **safety**. Peptides work **with** your body's natural processes rather than replacing them with synthetic hormones. This means you're less likely to experience the harsh side effects commonly associated with steroids.

Peptides like **BPC-157** and **TB-500** are especially popular because of their regenerative properties. They promote tissue repair, reduce inflammation, and can even speed up recovery from injuries—all without causing systemic imbalances in your body. Similarly, peptides like **CJC-1295** and **Ipamorelin** help stimulate growth hormone production without causing the hormonal swings that steroids can trigger.

Another big plus for peptides is that they're versatile. You're not just getting muscle growth; you're also getting benefits like **fat loss**, improved **skin health**, and even cognitive enhancement, depending on the peptide you choose.

Steroids: Potent but Risky

Steroids are undeniably powerful. If you're looking for rapid, dramatic gains in muscle mass and strength, steroids will deliver. **Testosterone**, **Dianabol**, and **Anadrol** are known for giving bodybuilders that edge in the gym, but they're not without risks.

Here are some common issues steroid users face:

- **Liver toxicity**: Oral steroids, in particular, can be hard on the liver. Over time, this can lead to liver damage or even failure.

- **Hormonal imbalances**: Since steroids replace your body's natural hormones, long-term use can shut down your natural hormone production. This can lead to issues like testicular atrophy or infertility.

- **Cardiovascular risks**: Steroids can mess with your cholesterol levels, raising **LDL (bad cholesterol)** and lowering **HDL (good cholesterol)**, which increases your risk of heart disease.

- **Psychological effects**: Steroids have been linked to mood swings, aggression (known as "roid rage"), and even long-term mental health problems like depression and anxiety.

The Verdict: Why Peptides Are the Smarter Choice

At the end of the day, peptides offer a more sustainable, long-term approach to performance enhancement and recovery. They work with your body rather than overpowering it, meaning you're less likely to experience dangerous side effects or long-term damage. **Steroids** might give you fast results, but peptides are the smarter, safer choice if you're in it for the long haul.

Steroids may have their place in short-term muscle building, but for most people—especially those who value health and longevity—peptides provide a safer, more versatile option. Whether you're looking to boost muscle growth, burn fat, or simply recover faster, peptides can help you get there without the risks that come with steroid use.

5

Featured Peptides

Featured Peptides

Alright, now that you've got a handle on the basics and know how peptides compare to steroids, let's dive into some of the most popular peptides out there. These aren't just buzzwords in the health and fitness world—each of these peptides has been studied for its unique properties and benefits. Whether you're looking to build muscle, shed fat, recover from an injury, or just age gracefully, these peptides have something to offer.

BPC-157

Overview: BPC-157 is like your body's repairman. Known for its healing and regenerative properties, this synthetic peptide is derived from a naturally occurring protein found in the stomach. It's used primarily for its ability to promote the healing of tissues, making it a favorite among athletes and those recovering from injuries.

Mechanism of Action: BPC-157 works by promoting **angiogenesis**, or the formation of new blood vessels, which is crucial for healing damaged tissues. It also boosts the production of **growth factors**, the molecules that help repair and regenerate muscle, tendons, ligaments, and even the gut lining. This peptide doesn't just patch things up—it actively supports your body's ability to heal itself faster and more effectively.

Benefits:

- Accelerates the healing of muscles, tendons, and ligaments

- Improves gut health by protecting the gut lining

- Reduces inflammation and speeds up recovery from injuries

- May have neuroprotective properties, potentially improving cognitive function

Dosage and Cycle: Most people take **250 mcg to 750 mcg daily**, injected subcutaneously or intramuscularly near the injury site. The typical cycle lasts for a few weeks to a couple of months, depending on the severity of the injury or condition.

Safety and Side Effects: BPC-157 is generally considered safe, with minimal side effects reported. Occasionally, people might experience mild gastrointestinal discomfort or headaches, but these effects are usually short-lived.

TB-500 (Thymosin Beta-4)

Overview: Next up is **TB-500**, another heavy-hitter when it comes to recovery. This peptide is naturally present in nearly every human cell and is a major player in healing and repair processes. It's especially popular among athletes dealing with muscle and tendon injuries, thanks to its powerful anti-inflammatory effects.

Mechanism of Action: TB-500 promotes **cell proliferation**, which basically means it helps your body create new cells to replace damaged ones. It also encourages **angiogenesis** (similar to BPC-157), speeding up tissue repair and reducing inflammation.

TB-500 is also known to improve flexibility in joints and tendons, reducing the risk of future injuries.

Benefits:

- Speeds up wound healing and tissue repair

- Reduces inflammation, particularly in joints and tendons

- Improves flexibility and reduces injury risk

- May support hair growth by improving follicle health

Dosage and Cycle: The typical dosage for TB-500 is **2-2.5 mg twice per week** during the initial 4-6 weeks, followed by a maintenance dose of **2-2.5 mg once per week**. This cycle can vary depending on your recovery needs.

Safety and Side Effects: TB-500 is generally well-tolerated with very few side effects. Some users report mild lethargy or a temporary head rush after administration, but these are typically short-lived.

Ipamorelin

Overview: If you're looking to increase your body's natural production of growth hormone, **Ipamorelin** is one of the best peptides to consider. This growth hormone secretagogue (GHS) is designed to stimulate the release of growth hormone from the pituitary gland, helping you build muscle, burn fat, and recover faster—all without the side effects associated with synthetic growth hormones.

Mechanism of Action: Ipamorelin works by mimicking the action of **ghrelin**, the hunger hormone, which binds to ghrelin receptors in the pituitary gland. This interaction stimulates the release of **growth hormone (GH)** in a natural, pulsatile manner, similar to how your body would produce GH on its own.

Benefits:

- Boosts growth hormone levels, aiding in muscle growth

- Enhances recovery and speeds up healing

- Supports fat loss, particularly in stubborn areas

- Provides anti-aging benefits by maintaining skin elasticity and youthful energy

Dosage and Cycle: The typical dosage for Ipamorelin is **200-300 mcg**, injected once or twice per day. Most users run cycles that last **8 to 12 weeks**, depending on their goals.

Safety and Side Effects: Ipamorelin is known for its mild side effects, with users reporting only occasional water retention or headaches. Unlike some other peptides, it doesn't significantly increase cortisol or prolactin levels, making it a safer option for those concerned about hormone imbalances.

Semaglutide

Overview: Originally designed to treat Type 2 diabetes, **Semaglutide** has become one of the most powerful tools for **weight management**. This GLP-1 receptor agonist works by reducing appetite and improving insulin sensitivity, making it a go-to for those looking to lose significant amounts of fat while improving their overall metabolic health.

Mechanism of Action: Semaglutide mimics the action of **GLP-1 (glucagon-like peptide-1)**, which enhances **insulin secretion**, reduces **glucagon release**, and slows down **gastric emptying**. Together, these effects help control hunger, improve blood sugar levels, and promote fat loss.

Benefits:

- Significant weight loss through appetite suppression

- Improved insulin sensitivity, great for those with metabolic disorders

- Enhanced glycemic control for managing blood sugar

- Long-lasting effects (weekly injections) make it convenient for sustained fat loss

Dosage and Cycle: Starting doses of Semaglutide typically range from **0.25 mg per week**, with a gradual increase to **1 mg per week** based on individual tolerance and results. It's often used for extended periods, with medical supervision, to achieve the desired fat loss.

Safety and Side Effects: While effective, Semaglutide can cause some side effects, especially in the beginning. Nausea, vomiting, and diarrhea are common but usually subside as your body gets used to the medication. Always consult a healthcare provider before starting a Semaglutide regimen.

6

Somatopause and Age-Related Weight Gain

Somatopause and Age-Related Weight Gain (Expanded)

Alright, now that we've covered the basics of peptides, let's talk about a specific issue that affects almost everyone as they get older—**somatopause**. If you're over 30 and wondering why the pounds seem to stick around a little longer and your energy levels are dipping, you're not imagining it. Somatopause is a natural decline in **growth hormone (GH)** production that happens as we age. The good news? Peptides can help.

What is Somatopause?

Somatopause is the fancy term for the **gradual decline of growth hormone** production that starts in your 30s and continues throughout your life. Growth hormone is responsible for many of the things we take for granted in our younger years—like building lean muscle, burning fat, and recovering quickly from workouts. When your GH levels drop, so do those perks.

By the time most people hit their 40s and 50s, they're producing **half the growth hormone** they did in their 20s. This drop in GH leads to several noticeable changes:

- **Fat accumulation**, especially around the midsection

- **Loss of muscle mass**

- **Decreased exercise effectiveness**

- **Slower metabolism**

- **Increased risk of cardiovascular disease**

- **Decline in cognitive function**

Basically, the same things we tend to chalk up to "getting older" are heavily influenced by somatopause. The lack of GH in your system makes it harder to stay lean, build muscle, and feel energized.

How Peptides Can Help with Somatopause

Here's where peptides come into play. Several peptides have been studied for their ability to **boost growth hormone levels**, helping to counteract the effects of somatopause. Unlike synthetic growth hormone injections, peptides **stimulate your body's natural production** of GH, leading to more stable and sustainable results.

Some of the key peptides used to combat somatopause include:

- **Sermorelin**: A popular **growth hormone-releasing hormone (GHRH)** analog that stimulates the pituitary gland to release more GH. It's often used to improve sleep, increase muscle mass, and burn fat.

- **CJC-1295**: Another **GHRH** that works similarly to Sermorelin but with a longer half-life. CJC-1295 is often combined with **Ipamorelin** to increase the pulse frequency of GH release, mimicking the body's natural rhythm.

- **GHRP-2 and GHRP-6: Growth hormone-releasing peptides (GHRP)** that stimulate the pituitary gland to secrete GH. GHRP-6 is known for stimulating appetite, while GHRP-2 focuses more on boosting GH without the appetite increase.

- **Ipamorelin**: A **GH secretagogue** that mimics the body's natural GH release without affecting other hormones like cortisol or prolactin. It's a favorite for those looking to boost muscle growth, recovery, and fat loss without harsh side effects.

Peptides for Fat Loss and Muscle Preservation

In addition to increasing GH, some peptides are specifically designed to **target fat loss** and **preserve muscle mass**, both of which are key to fighting age-related weight gain. These peptides include:

- **Fragment 176-191**: A synthetic peptide derived from GH that focuses specifically on fat loss. It helps **break down fat cells** and can be a powerful tool for burning stubborn fat around the waistline.

- **AOD9604**: This peptide is also a **fat-burning fragment** of GH. It's designed to stimulate **lipolysis** (fat breakdown) without affecting blood sugar levels or causing muscle loss.

- **MOTS-c** and **5-Amino-1MQ**: These peptides work on the **cellular level** to increase metabolism, improve mitochondrial function, and promote fat burning. They're particularly useful for people experiencing a slow metabolism due to aging.

Managing Appetite and Cravings

One of the toughest parts about aging is controlling your appetite and cravings. That's where peptides like **Semaglutide** and **Tirzepatide** come in. Both peptides are **GLP-1 receptor agonists**, which means they help reduce appetite and control cravings by slowing down gastric emptying and improving insulin sensitivity.

In fact, **Semaglutide** has become a popular option for weight management, with studies showing significant weight loss when used alongside a calorie-controlled diet. It's an effective tool for reducing food intake and improving overall metabolic health, making it easier to maintain a lean physique as you age.

How Peptides Fight Age-Related Weight Gain

By addressing the underlying hormonal and metabolic changes that occur with aging, peptides offer a multi-faceted approach to **combating age-related weight gain**. They help by:

- Increasing **growth hormone** levels, which boosts muscle mass and burns fat.

- Promoting **fat burning** at the cellular level through peptides like **Fragment 176-191** and **AOD9604**.

- Managing appetite and cravings with **GLP-1 agonists** like Semaglutide.

- Improving **metabolism** and mitochondrial function with peptides like **MOTS-c** and **5-Amino-1MQ**.

In short, peptides help reverse many of the effects of somatopause, making it easier to maintain a healthy weight, build muscle, and stay energized—no matter how many birthdays you've celebrated.

7

The Peptide Revolution

The Peptide Revolution

We've already covered a lot of ground, but now it's time to take a step back and look at the bigger picture—the **Peptide Revolution**. Peptides aren't just a passing trend; they're at the forefront of a new era in health, wellness, and performance. From their use in elite sports to cutting-edge medical therapies, peptides are becoming a cornerstone of modern science. And here's the exciting part—we're just getting started.

Beyond Muscle and Fat Loss

When most people think of peptides, they immediately think of building muscle, losing fat, and recovering faster from workouts. And sure, that's a huge part of why peptides are so popular in the fitness community, but the truth is that peptides have far-reaching applications beyond just performance enhancement.

According to the **Peptide Therapy Guide**, peptides are being used in a wide range of treatments, including:

- **Cancer therapies**: Certain peptides are being studied for their ability to target cancer cells more precisely than traditional treatments like chemotherapy. By attaching to specific receptors on cancer cells, peptides could potentially deliver therapeutic compounds directly to the tumor without damaging healthy tissue.

- **Organ and tissue repair**: Peptides like **BPC-157** and **TB-500** are not only popular among athletes but are also being studied for their role in healing internal organs. These peptides could help repair damaged liver, heart, or kidney tissue, providing a new way to treat chronic conditions.

- **Immune system support**: Peptides like **Thymosin Alpha-1** are being used to **boost immune function** and help fight off infections. In a world where immune health is more important than ever, peptides may offer a way to strengthen the body's defenses naturally.

- **Anti-inflammatory treatments**: Peptides have shown great potential in treating chronic inflammation, which is linked to conditions like arthritis, heart disease, and even Alzheimer's. Peptides like **BPC-157** and **TB-500** are being studied for their ability to reduce inflammation and promote healing at the same time.

- **Anti-aging therapies**: Perhaps one of the most exciting areas of peptide research is in the field of **anti-aging**. Peptides like **Epitalon** and **GH secretagogues** are being studied for their ability to extend lifespan and improve quality of life as we age. Imagine living into your 70s or 80s with the energy and vitality you had in your 30s— that's the goal of many peptide researchers.

The Future of Aging

The potential of peptides goes far beyond just weight loss and muscle growth. We're talking about **redefining aging**. Researchers are already looking into peptides that could help keep you younger, not just in how you look, but in how you feel and function. Peptides like **Epitalon** work by regulating the **telomeres**—the protective caps at the ends of your chromosomes. Shorter telomeres are associated with aging, and peptides that target telomere maintenance could be a game-changer in slowing down the aging process.

Peptides are also being studied for their **cognitive benefits**. **Cerebrolysin**, for example, is a peptide that's been researched for its ability to **protect brain cells** and improve memory and cognitive function. This kind of research could lead to treatments for neurodegenerative diseases like **Alzheimer's** and **Parkinson's**, offering hope for millions of people.

What Does This Mean for You?

You don't have to wait for the future to start benefiting from peptides. The Peptide Revolution is happening right now, and more people are catching on to how these tiny molecules can make a big difference in their lives. From boosting athletic performance to enhancing recovery, improving skin elasticity, and even potentially extending lifespan—peptides are the real deal.

So what's next? As research continues, we're likely to see even more peptides hit the market, each one designed to target a specific issue, whether it's disease, aging, or performance. The beauty of peptides is that they can be highly specialized, meaning you're not just treating symptoms—you're addressing the root cause of the issue at a cellular level.

A Word of Caution

While the potential of peptides is incredibly exciting, it's important to approach them with the right mindset. Yes, peptides can offer amazing benefits, but they're not a magic bullet. It's essential to consult with a healthcare professional before starting any new peptide regimen, especially if you're dealing with a chronic health condition or taking other medications.

Remember, the Peptide Revolution is all about optimizing your health and performance, but it works best when combined with a balanced lifestyle. Proper diet, exercise, sleep, and stress management will always be foundational to your health—peptides are just the icing on the cake.

8

Where to Buy Peptides

Where to Buy Peptides

By now, you're probably wondering where you can actually get your hands on these powerful peptides. When it comes to purchasing peptides, quality and purity are everything. You don't want to mess around with substandard products that could be ineffective—or worse, unsafe. Luckily, there are some reputable sources that provide high-quality peptides that you can trust.

Why Quality Matters

Not all peptides are created equal. The peptide market is largely unregulated, which means it's up to you to find a trusted supplier. You'll want to look for peptides that are **third-party tested**, with verified **purity levels above 99%**. This ensures that what you're injecting into your body is exactly what it says on the label—no fillers, no contaminants, just pure, effective peptide.

Also, keep an eye out for **Certificates of Analysis (COA)**. These are lab reports that detail the exact contents of a peptide product. Reputable suppliers will make these available for every batch they sell. If a supplier isn't transparent about testing or doesn't provide COAs, that's a red flag.

The Amino Source: A Trusted Provider

When it comes to reliable peptide suppliers, **The Amino Source** is one name you can trust. They've built a solid reputation for providing high-quality, third-party-tested peptides that meet the strictest standards for purity and effectiveness.

Here's why **The Amino Source** stands out:

- **Purity Guaranteed**: Every peptide sold is third-party tested for purity, and their products always exceed **99% purity**. This ensures that you're getting exactly what you pay for, with no harmful additives.

- **Detailed Certificates of Analysis**: They provide **COAs** for every product batch, so you can see exactly what's in your peptide before you inject it.

- **Customer Support**: Got questions? Their knowledgeable customer support team is available to help guide you through the process of selecting and using peptides.

- **Educational Resources**: Whether you're new to peptides or just want to learn more, their website is packed with valuable information, including **how-to guides**, **dosing recommendations**, and more.

How to Order from The Amino Source

Purchasing peptides from **The Amino Source** is simple. You can visit their website at www.TheAminoSource.com and browse through their selection of peptides. They carry everything from the healing powers of **BPC-157** and **TB-500**, to **fat-burning peptides** like **AOD9604**, and **growth hormone secretagogues** like **CJC-1295** and **Ipamorelin**.

Once you've made your selection, you can easily place your order online. And, they provide detailed usage instructions and mixing materials with each order, making it easier for you to get started with your peptide regimen.

9

Conclusion and Resources

Conclusion and Resources

We've covered a lot of ground in this guide—from the basics of peptides to their revolutionary applications in health, fitness, and longevity. By now, you should have a solid understanding of how peptides work, how to use them safely, and what they can do for your body.

Whether you're looking to **build muscle**, **burn fat**, **recover faster**, or even **slow down the aging process**, peptides offer a versatile, safe, and effective solution. Unlike synthetic steroids or traditional hormone replacement therapies, peptides work with your body's natural systems, making them a smarter choice for long-term health and performance.

But remember, while peptides can deliver incredible results, they're not a magic pill. You still need to put in the work—maintaining a balanced diet, exercising regularly, getting enough sleep, and managing your stress levels will always be the foundation of good health. Peptides are simply another tool in your arsenal to help you optimize your body and reach your goals.

Resources to Keep Learning

If you're ready to take the next step in your peptide journey, here are some valuable resources to help you stay informed and make educated decisions:

- **Scientific Journals**: For those who love to dive into the data, journals like **The Journal of Clinical Endocrinology & Metabolism** and **Neuropsychopharmacology** regularly publish research on peptides and their applications in medicine, sports, and aging.

- **Educational Websites**: Websites like **MedlinePlus** and **PubMed** provide reliable, research-backed information about peptides and other health topics. These are great resources for learning about the science behind peptide therapies.

- **Community Forums**: If you're looking for real-world experiences and community support, forums like **Evolutionary.org** and **r/Peptides** on Reddit are filled with people who have used peptides and are willing to share their insights. But always take personal anecdotes with a grain of salt—everyone's body reacts differently to peptides, and it's important to verify any advice with scientific sources.

Final Thoughts

The peptide revolution is here, and the possibilities are endless. Whether you're an athlete looking to maximize your performance, someone recovering from injury, or just someone trying to keep the inevitable effects of aging at bay, peptides can be a game-changer. But like any powerful tool, they need to be used correctly. Always do your research, source your peptides from reputable suppliers, and consult with a healthcare professional before starting any new regimen.

So, what's next? That's up to you. Armed with the knowledge from this guide, you're now ready to explore the world of peptides and take your health, performance, and longevity to the next level.

Peptide	Use	Recommended Dosage	Amount in Vial	Recommended amount of BAC Water to reconstitute entire vial	Units in syringe (Type of syringe, Amount of pull)	Frequency
Semaglutide GLP-1	Weight Loss Physician Care Required	.25 MG (Increase dose every 4 weeks until you arrive at the right dose. MAX 2.4 MG)	10 MG	2 ml	0.5 ml, pull the syringe to the 10	Once per week, same day each week.

Tirzepatide GLP-1, GIP	Weight Loss Physician Care Required	2.5 Mg (Increase dose every 4 weeks until you arrive at the right dose. MAX 10 MG without a doctor monitoring)	10 MG	2 ml	1 ml, pull the syringe to 20	Once per week, same day each week.
Retatrutide GLP-1, GIP, Glucagon	Weight Loss Physician Care Required	Testing has been down at 2 MG, 4 MG, 8 MG and 12 MG. Average dose 2 - 5 MG	10 MG	2 ml	1 ml, pull the syringe to 40 for 2 mg, 80 for 4 mg.	Once per week, same day each week.
MOTS-C	Weight Loss Swift deterioration - unsuitable for storage	5 MG 10 MG Best in belly fat	5 MG 10 MG	1 ML 1 ML	1 ml, pull the syringe to 100	3X/week (M,W,F) 1X/Week

MOTS - C / Humanin Blend	Weight Loss	5 MG / 5 MG	5 MG / 5 MG	1 ML	1 ml, pull the syringe to 100	Every 3rd day (M,W,F) 4 - 6 weeks then 1X/Wk 5MG Dose for 4 weeks
5 - Amino - 1- MQ	Weight Loss , Energy, Boots Metabo lism, Activat es the Longevi ty Gene	50,100, 150 MG	50 MG Cap			1X/Day AM with food for absorptio n 20-30 days on, 1 - 2 weeks off
Tesofensine	Weight Loss, Cogniti on	500 MCG, 250 MCG, 125 MCG	Cap			1X/Day AM After 3-6 Mo. Cycle off for a month
Ipamorelin HGH Analogue	Weight Loss, Healing Soft Tissue, Brain, Sleep, Muscle Buildin g, Beauty	100 - 500 MCG	10 MG	3 ML	1 ML, Pull syringe as follows: 100 = 3, 200 = 6, 250 = 7.5	1 - 3X/Day - Goal Matters 5 Days On, 2 Off 6 - 8 Weeks On 6 - 8 Weeks Off

AOD - 9604	Weight Loss	300 MCG 1X/Day Or 250 MCG 2X/Day	10 MG	2 ML	1 ml, pull the syringe to 6 for 300 MCG, pull the syringe to 5 for 250 MCG	1X/Day or 2X/Day
BPC - 157 / TB4 Fragment 17-23	Healing Soft Tissue, Cut, Brain	400 MCG BPC / 2 MG TB4 200 MCG BPC / 1 MG TB4	10 MG / 50 MG 10 MG / 25 MG	3 ML	1 ML, pull the syringe to 12	30 Day Cycle or 8 Weeks on / Off
BPC 157	Healing Soft Tissue	.5 MG / 1 MG	10 MG	2 ML	1 ML, Pull the syringe to 10 for .5 MG, Pull to 20 for 1 MG	Once a day
TB-500	Muscle Growth, Healing Soft Tissue	2 MG	10 MG	2 ML	1 ML, Pull syringe to 40 for 2 MG	2X/WK for injury evenly spaced out 4 - 6 weeks on 2 weeks off

HCG 5000iu	Muscle Growth, Fertility	250iu	5000iu	1 ML	1 ML, Pull syringe to 5	3X/WK Double the dosage for fertility use
Melanotan 2	Brain, Tan, Immunity	Brain 250 MCG Tan/Imm unity 200 MCG Adjust dose based on pigment changes	10 MG	1 ML	1 ML, Pull syringe to 2.5 for 250 MCG, pull to 2 for 200 MCG	Brain 1-2X/WK Tan Daily for 7 days Immunity Daily
PT-141	Sexual Health	Women - 1.5 MG Men - 2.0 MG	10 MG	1 ML	1 ml, pull the syringe to 15 for 1.5 mg, 20 for 2 mg.	8X/Month Do Not Overuse
Semax	Brain Restoration, Energy	300 MCG - 1000 MCG	10 ML	100 MCG Per Spray 3 - 10 Sprays		1 - 3X/ Day
Adamax	Brain Restoration, Energy	100 MCG - 200 MCG Never Over 300 MCG		100 MCG Per Spray 1 - 2 Sprays		1 - 2X/ Day

Oxytocin	Brain, Sleep, Immunity, Weight Loss, Sexual Health	100 MCG - 1000 MCG		100 MCG Per Spray 1 - 10 Sprays		1 - 3X/ Day
P-21	Brain Restoration (Cognition)	100 MCG - 1000 MCG		100 MCG Per Spray 1 - 10 Sprays Mot People Avg 3 - 7 Sprays		1 - 3X/ Day
DSIP	Brain, Sleep, Longevity	100 MCG - 150 MCG	10 MG	2 ML	1 ml, pull the syringe to 2 for 100 MCG, pull the syringe to 3 for 150 MCG	Max 15X/MO
KPV	Brain, Wound Healing, Immunity, Anti-Inflammitory	200 MCG - 500 MCG	10 MG	2 ML	1 ml, Pull the syringe to: 4 for 200 MCG 6 for 300 MCG 8 for 400 MCG 10 for 500 MCG	Once in the AM until resolved

IPAMORELIN / CJC-1295 Blend HGH Analogue	Increase Muscle Mass, Burn Fat, Sleep Quality, Bone Density, Skin Elasticity	200 MCG IPA / 200 MCG CJC-1295	10 MG / 10 MG	3 ML	1 ml, Pull the syringe to 6 for 200/200	5 Days On, Two Days Off 6 - 8 Weeks On 6 - 8 Weeks Off
CJC-1295 W/O DAC HGH Analogue	Increase Muscle Mass, Burn Fat, Sleep Quality, Bone Density, Skin Elasticity	200 MCG	10 MG	3 ML	1 ml, Pull the syringe to 6 for 200	5 Days On, Two Days Off 6 - 8 Weeks On 6 - 8 Weeks Off
TESAMORELIN HGH Analogue	Brain, Increase Muscle Mass, Burn Fat, Sleep Quality, Bone Density,	1 MG	5 MG	1 ML	1 ml, Pull the syringe to 20 for with 1 MG	1 - 2x/ day, 5 Days per Week 6 - 8 Weeks On 6 - 8 Weeks Off

TA1	Immunity, Regeneration	1.5 MG - 2 MG	10 MG	1 ML	1 ml, Pull the syringe to 15 for 1.5 MG 20 for 2 MG	2X/ Week for 8 Weeks On, 8 Weeks Off 5 Days On, 2 Days Off
BPC-157, KPV, Larazotide	Gut, Regeneration, Immunity, Brain	250 MCG 250 MCG 125 MCG		With or Without Food	AM	1X/Day
VIP	Immunity, Digestion, Blood Flow	50 MCG	5 MG	5 ML	Pull the Syringe to 5 for 50 MCG	30 - 90 Days
LL-37	Immunity, Antimicrobial	125 MCG	5 MG	2 ML	1 ml, Pull the Syringe to 5 for 125 MCG	30 Days On, 2 Weeks Off
GHK-Cu	Cosmetic, Wound Healing, Pain Reduction	5 MG (5000 MCG)	200 MG	4 ML	1 ml, Pull the syringe to 10 for 5 MG	5 - 30 Days on, 30 Days Cycle Off

SELANK	Memory Improvement, Anxiety and Depression Reduction, Stress Reduction, Improve Attention Span	300 - 1000 MCG	10 ML	300 MCG per spray	1 - 3 Sprays	2 - 4 Weeks Minimum. 12 Weeks Best for Trial
FGL	Improve Congnitive Function, Memory and Learning	1 - 2 MG	10 MG	1 ML	1 ml, Pull the Syringe to 10 for 1 MG Pull the Syringe to 20 for 2 MG	5 Days On, 2 Days Off
CEREBROLYSIN	Brain Repair, Dementia, Stroke, Craniocerebral Trauma	5 or 10 ML	20 ML	2 ML	1 ml, Pull the Syringe to 50 for 5 ML Pull the Syringe to 100 for 10 ML	10 - 20 Days

| THYMALIN | Longevity, Inflammation | 5 MG | 20 MG | 2 ML | 1 ml, Pull the Syringe to 50 for 5 MG | 1X for 20 Days Only Do Once every 6 Months |
| EPITALON | Longevity, Anti-Aging | 10 MG | 20 MG | 1 ML | 1 ml, Pull the Syringe to 50 for 10 MG | 10 Days in a row or 3X/Week for 3 Consecutive Weeks

Not more than 2X/ Year |